William Scott 1950s Nude Drawings

William SCOTT

1950s Nude Drawings

Karsten Schubert

Ridinghouse

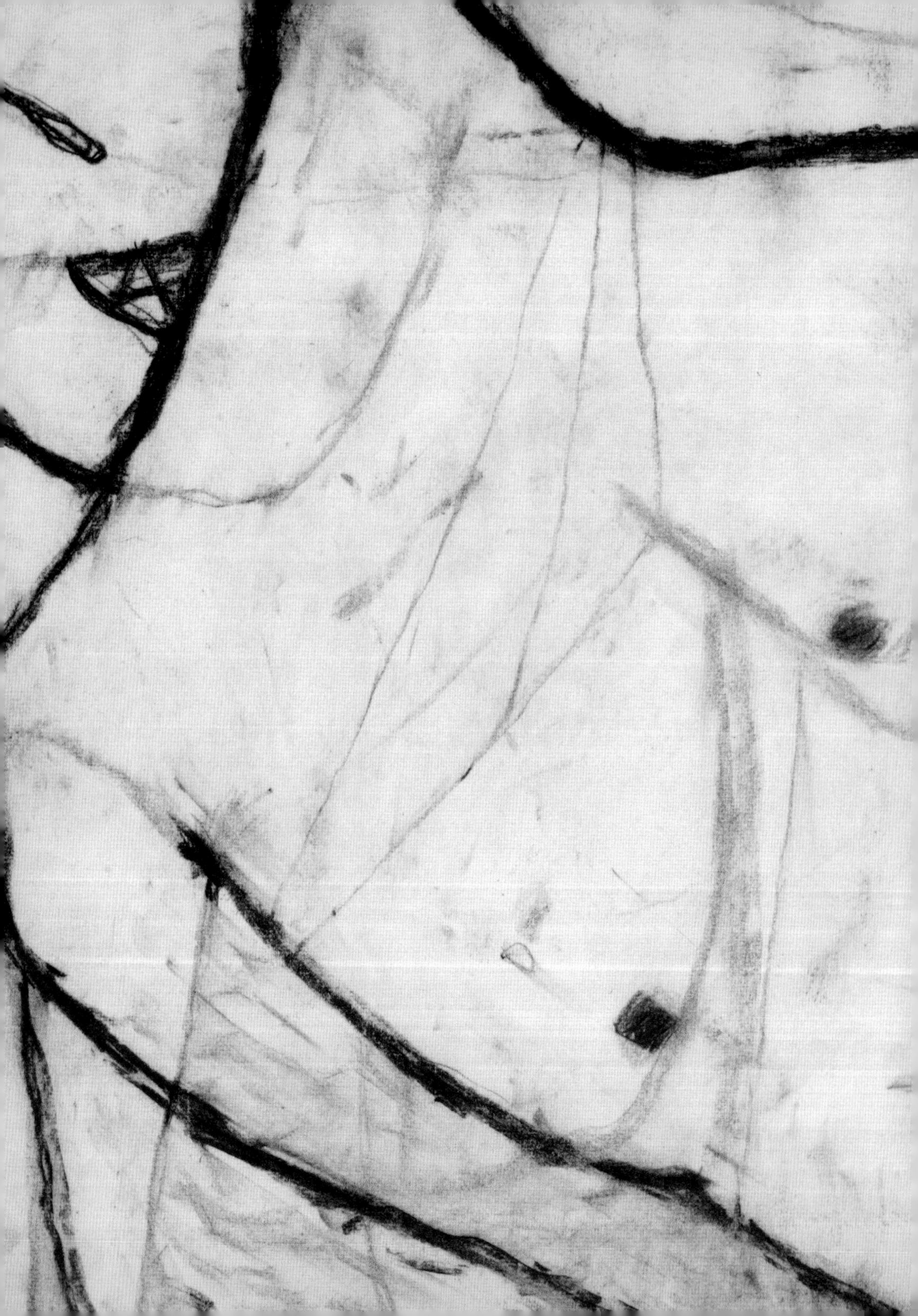

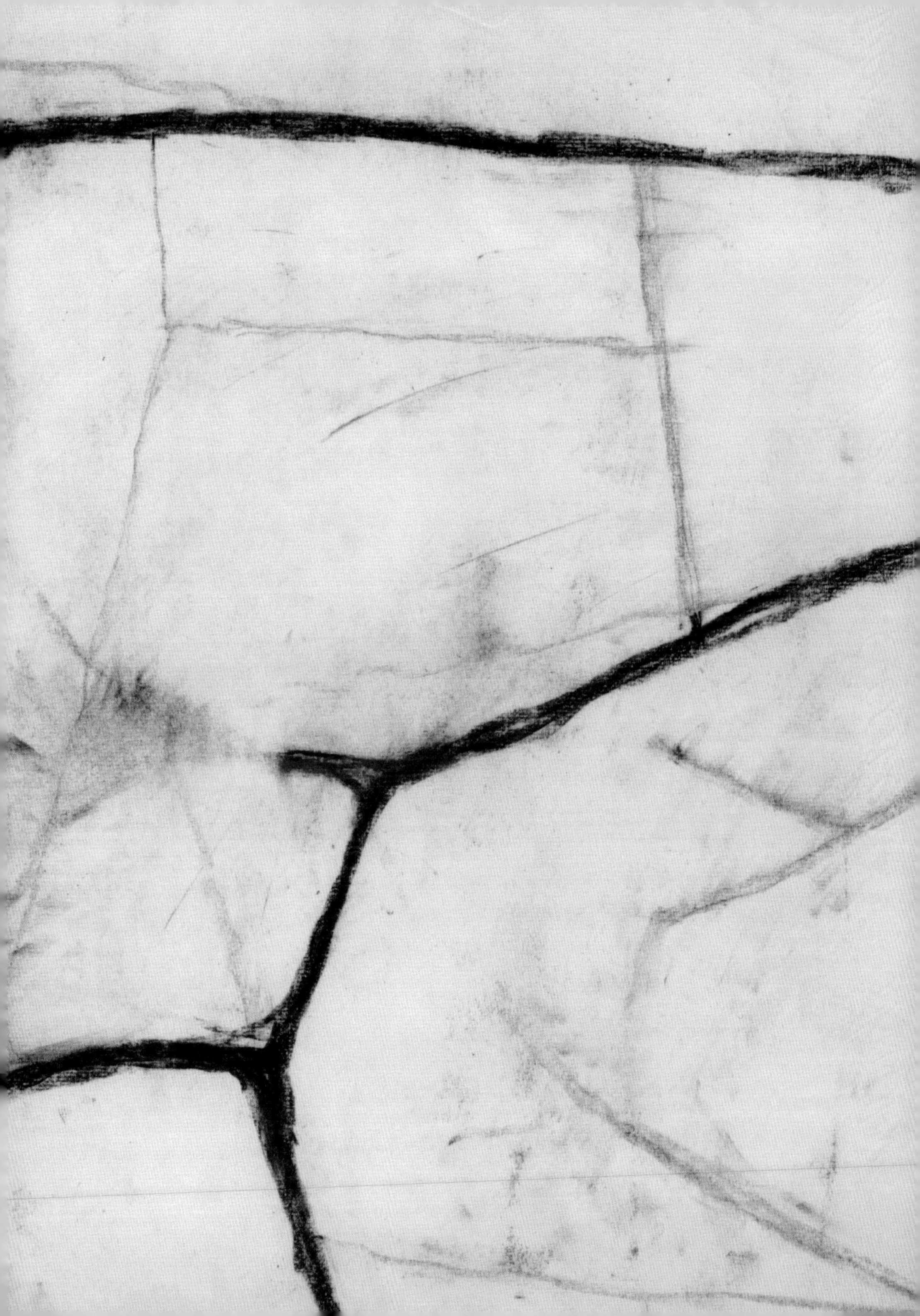

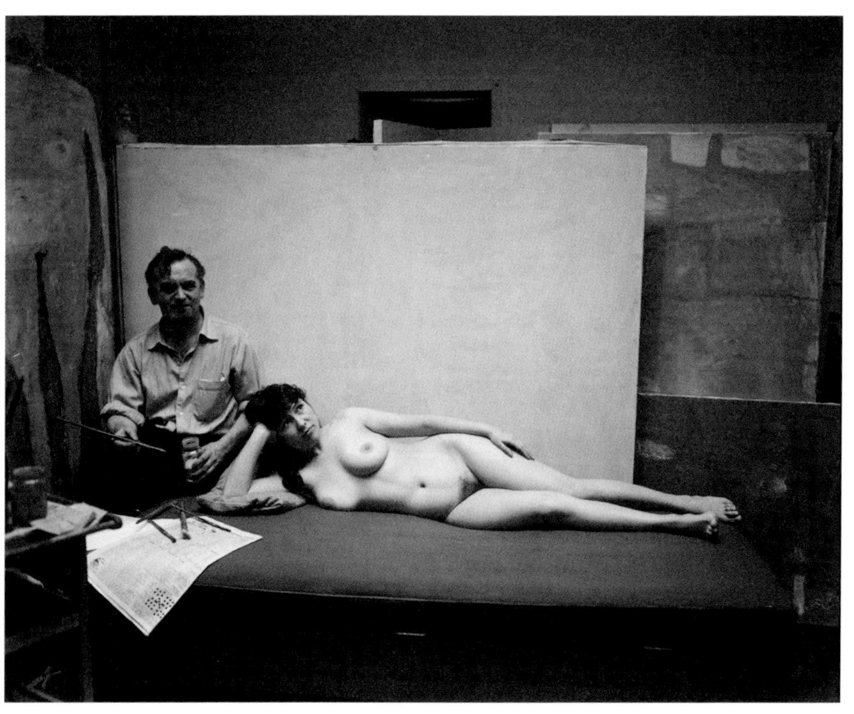

The artist and model, 1956

Disconcerting Contours Sarah Whitfield

I have all my life considered myself as being a figure painter.
– Letter from William Scott to an unidentified friend, 'George', 24 February 1952

One of William Scott's earliest memories was playing hopscotch on the pavements of Greenock, the port on the River Clyde where he was born: 'In the summer we played on the streets in our bare feet, the pavement and walls covered in chalk patterns on which we jumped and skipped.' The soft marks left by chalk on an abrasive surface such as a pavement are as imprecise as those left by charcoal on a sheet of white paper. Untitled – Nude (1956; p.16), for example, is a drawing filled with the history of its making through a tangle of scuffed, smudged and half-erased lines still visible beneath the image. These grey ghosts give the drawing a depth and a texture equivalent to Scott's works in oils in which the paint is built up in unevenly applied layers; every shift in the composition, every little change of mind, is left deliberately exposed.

Scott, like many artists before him, had a horror of the blank piece of paper, of the emptiness of an untouched canvas. 'It is so shocking to me', he once wrote, 'that I am forced to scrawl on it with charcoal.' Charcoal, like chalk, is hard to erase without leaving a grimy trail of grey-black, but then, the messiness of the medium was what Scott liked and encouraged. The sight of 'a thing well done', as he put it, was disturbing. One stroke of his charcoal stick and the furred line it left behind took the sting out of the whiteness and helped to allay – one may imagine – that initial fear of the pristine surface. Once the threat had been overcome, Scott could go on to make a drawing that in its clarity and restraint seems, perversely, to recover the purity he had set out to destroy.

The drawings in the present exhibition were realised between 1953 and 1956,
a period when Scott was fighting against what he called 'the recognisable image from
the kitchen', a reference to his still life subjects of the late 1940s in which the frying
pan and other pots and pans from the modest kitchens of his youth take centre stage.
His pictures, as he said himself, had been growing steadily greyer, until he was using
just black and white 'with subtleties of green and yellow'. Drawing allowed him to
think in the simplified terms of black and white and relieved him, so he claimed,
'of responsibilities and struggles with colour'. The magnificent series of near abstract
drawings, of which *Seated Woman* (1953; p.20) is a prime example, shows how he began
to solve the problem of the image by finding a space between the figurative and the
abstract. Perhaps this is what Scott meant when he told his friend Lawrence Alloway
about his preoccupation with 'the modern magic of space', meaning, one could say,
the acceptance of the flat canvas and the banishment of perspective as prerequisites
for painting. He went on to list his other preoccupations: 'primitive sex forms, the
sensual and erotic, disconcerting contours, the things of life.'

In the paintings, a female figure stretched the length of a canvas could be read
as a landscape or a tabletop, the illusion of all three images endlessly slipping one
between the other. It was the sort of ambiguity Scott saw in the half-forgotten
meanings of ancient signs and pictographs. On a visit to New York in August 1953 he
had seen at first hand one of Willem de Kooning's 'Woman' paintings in progress (and
had himself photographed in front of it). Shortly before that he had learned about
Dubuffet's series of heavily erotic female nudes, their ample, splayed bodies as ancient
in their appearance as the bulbous *Venus of Willendorf*. No wonder then, that in the
years immediately following both these major encounters, Scott appropriated the
female body. It was a way of freeing himself up technically as well as imaginatively,
but it also showed he now had the confidence not to fight his natural gifts as a
draughtsman.

It is not that long ago that Gustave Courbet's painting, *L'Origine du Monde*
(1866), was allowed to be seen in public, so it is easy to imagine how liberating it must
have been for Scott to make his own version of this unabashedly erotic subject, even if
the drawing in question, *Untitled – Reclining Nude* (1956; p.30), stops short of Courbet's

audacity. But what is so striking about this drawing is not so much the eroticism but the spatial use of line. The pose, which is so shockingly frank in Courbet's painting, becomes a means of creating a form as solidly made as a large china bowl. Solid though it is, it also opens up a space in the middle of the composition, a device Scott learned from Pierre Bonnard, the painter he admired almost more than any other, and which is seen in several of these drawings, Untitled [Nude] (1956; p.18) for example. The lines support the body like a wire armature. The torso of *Seated Woman* is so minimally drawn that it can be read as a space that has been emptied out, leaving a form that is weightless. Instead, and against visual logic, the torso appears solid, even fleshy. (Scott's early formation as a sculptor is usually visible in his figures, especially at this period.) Scott is also one of the few artists of his generation to understand that the line between the erotic and the comic is often indistinguishable (as de Kooning knew very well). And there is something wonderfully comic about Nude; her brashness, her flaunting pose, to say nothing of the single stocking, as though she has not had time to discard her last bit of clothing.

Scott loved the female body. He photographed his models and was photographed with them (p.6). He drew them constantly, and when there was no model to hand, turned to illustrations from books or magazines, or to his collection of postcards. In the text for the lecture on drawing he gave in Perth, Australia, in 1973 (see p.10) he quoted Ingres as saying: 'Draw all the time, draw with your eyes when you cannot draw with a pencil.' As these drawings show, Scott took that advice to heart. His nudes, however abstract, however classical, however uncompromising, have been drawn with the eyes every bit as much as they have with a stick of charcoal.

Lecture by William Scott, on the occasion of the Perth Prize for Drawing International, Perth, Australia, 1973

Drawing is an activity as old as man, it dates from the moment of discovery of pigment, powdered-clay combined with water could make marks of magic, a game that was to become the record of the history of mankind.

Earth, stone, water, fat, burnt-wood, papyrus, pottery, skin, paper, gum, graphite and ink became the media used to tell his story.

The story continues in this exhibition. I must confess that I am not too sure that I or anyone else can confidently go around and say here is the first, second and third best drawing, the race is now over and we know the winner; yet such exhibitions are a means to stimulate and to encourage the artist, the awards it should be remembered, could be reversed by another jury. I am full of praise for those who initiated an exhibition specifically for drawing. Drawing as a subject remained for a long time a private occupation of the artist, each artist had his own specific reason why he drew, but for many artists of the present time drawing is considered a complete entity of its own.

Before coming out to Perth knowing I was to be confronted with the complexity of diverse views on 'what is drawing?', there had been in London at the British Museum an exhibition covering 12,000 years of drawing, to the end of the nineteenth century. I thought it might be interesting to not only look at some of these drawings, but to find out what the artist over the course of time had to say about the activity of drawing, its reason and purpose.

Unfortunately nothing is recorded by the ancients, no note for us was left in Lascaux Caves to explain those beautiful drawings; we must almost wait until Leonardo da Vinci wrote his learned *Treatise of the Art of Drawing and Painting*.

Leonardo was in some respects remarkably near to our twentieth-century interest in new materials and technology. Being a scientist he offers practical help and advice such as I will quote. Three of his wise instructions to young artists are:

1. 'If you wish to draw from nature, you should be three times as far from the object you are drawing as it is high.'

2. 'If you wish to find profitable recreation in games choose them so they will be of use to you in your profession, that is, useful in forming the judgement of the eye in evaluating lengths and widths of objects.'

3. 'If you look at walls covered with many stains or made of stones of different colours, with the idea of imagining some scene, you will see in it landscapes adorned with mountains, rivers, rocks, trees, plains, broad valleys and hills of all kinds. You may also see in it battles and figures with lively gestures, or strange faces and costumes and an infinity of things which you can reduce to separate and complete forms.'

Any comment on this is unnecessary when we think of our recent Tachist, action painting and scraffito inspired modern art. If Leonardo was the judge today I wonder what artists he would award the prize to?

After Leonardo, I quote Michelangelo. He says, 'drawing is the fount and body of painting, sculpture, architecture and every other kind of art, the root of all the sciences. Let whoever may have attained to so much as to have the power of drawing, know that he holds a great treasure.' No doubt a very comfortable thought for any of us who might pride ourselves on the power of drawing.

I will remind you that Raphael as a young man drawing in a straight and stiff manner changed his taste at the sight of Michelangelo's works and became an ardent disciple.

I, personally, much admire the drawings of Ingres and I believe that [a lot of] modern as well as academic art has stemmed from his work. I believe that he has influenced much modern art.

1. 'Draw all the time, draw with your eyes when you cannot draw with a pencil.'

2. 'Drawing is the probity of art.'

3. 'Drawing includes everything except colour. It is the expression, the interior form, the plan, the modelling.'

4. 'The line is drawing, that is all.'

5. 'Smoke itself should be expressed by a line.'

6. 'There is neither correct nor incorrect drawing. There is only beautiful or ugly drawing.'

7. 'Draw with purity but also with breadth. Pure and broad, that is drawing, that is art.'

I have said enough about the distant past, I want to say something about the recent past. Van Gogh for me is the beginning of modern drawing. This was a conclusion I arrived at from an early work of his which was shown at the British Museum included in nineteenth-century drawing. A typical drawing of a landscape drawn with what looked to me like the mark of ink with a quill, a mosaic of deft touches, an all-overness containing a unity, though in monochrome it expressed his great power of colour.

Some artists have this strange quality of being able to transmute by line, dots, scratches and scribbles a sense of light which is also colour, a way of drawing given to us by Turner through the Impressionists. Van Gogh, though he wrote much, said little about drawing, but one of the interesting remarks he made was 'I consider the making of studies as sowing and the making of paintings as reaping.'

When I was a student there was a very strong conviction at the art school that the modern master of drawing was Degas. The direct descendent and heir of Ingres, he was in a sense a teacher and had a great many things to say about drawing that indeed were profound and traditional but true.

His statement that 'art cannot be made with intent to please' may have a good deal of truth. He also says, 'drawing is not form, it is a way of seeing form'. Drawing is not what you see but what you must make others see. From Italy to Spain, from Greece to Japan, there is not much difference of technique; everywhere it is a question of summing up life in its essential gestures and the rest is the business of the artist's eye and hand.

The British have perhaps not been notable much in the past for drawing as an abstract idea, the strong desire to illustrate by many of our artists and our strong concern with landscape reduced a great deal of our drawing to a high level of topographical draughtsmanship. But I am always fascinated with the fact that in the eighteenth century Alexander Cozens wrote a book describing a 'New Method of Landscape Composition'. He proposes in detail how the use of the blot can be so used with the use of black ink that blot-drawing can become an art form, anticipating by over 150 years our new large canvases of blots on sheets of sail cloth.

To know how to draw does not mean to draw well. Let us examine the famous science of draughtsmanship we hear so much about. Every Prix de Rome winner has that science at his fingertips but so have the competitors who come in last.

That remark was made by Gauguin, he also said, 'I have a horror of all this cookery needed to make a drawing.' This remark helps me to understand what his painting was about.

Conflict of expression there must be in art and each one of us must have his own taste, example: Redon says 'one must respect black, nothing prostitutes it. It does not please the eye or awaken another sense. It is the agent of the mind even more than the beautiful colour of the palette or the prism.' A sheet of white paper horrifies me. It is so shocking to me that I am forced to scrawl on it with charcoal. This operation brings it to life.

Matisse says, 'Once I have put my emotion to line and modelled the light of my white paper, without destroying its endearing whiteness, I can add or take away nothing further.'

The breadth of ideas which are now accepted as drawing is clearly shown in this exhibition. My preamble was to try to show that interpretation of drawing looked at over a span of years leads one to the conclusion that there were always many ways of drawing. Of the many quotations I made from our forebears the one I like best is Ingres when he says, 'there is neither correct or incorrect drawing; there is only beautiful or ugly drawing'.

I hope that I have had the perception out here in Perth of having chosen the beautiful.

William Scott 1950s Nude Drawings

Untitled – Nude, 1956
Charcoal on paper
94.5 × 62.5 cm | 37¼ × 24⅝ in

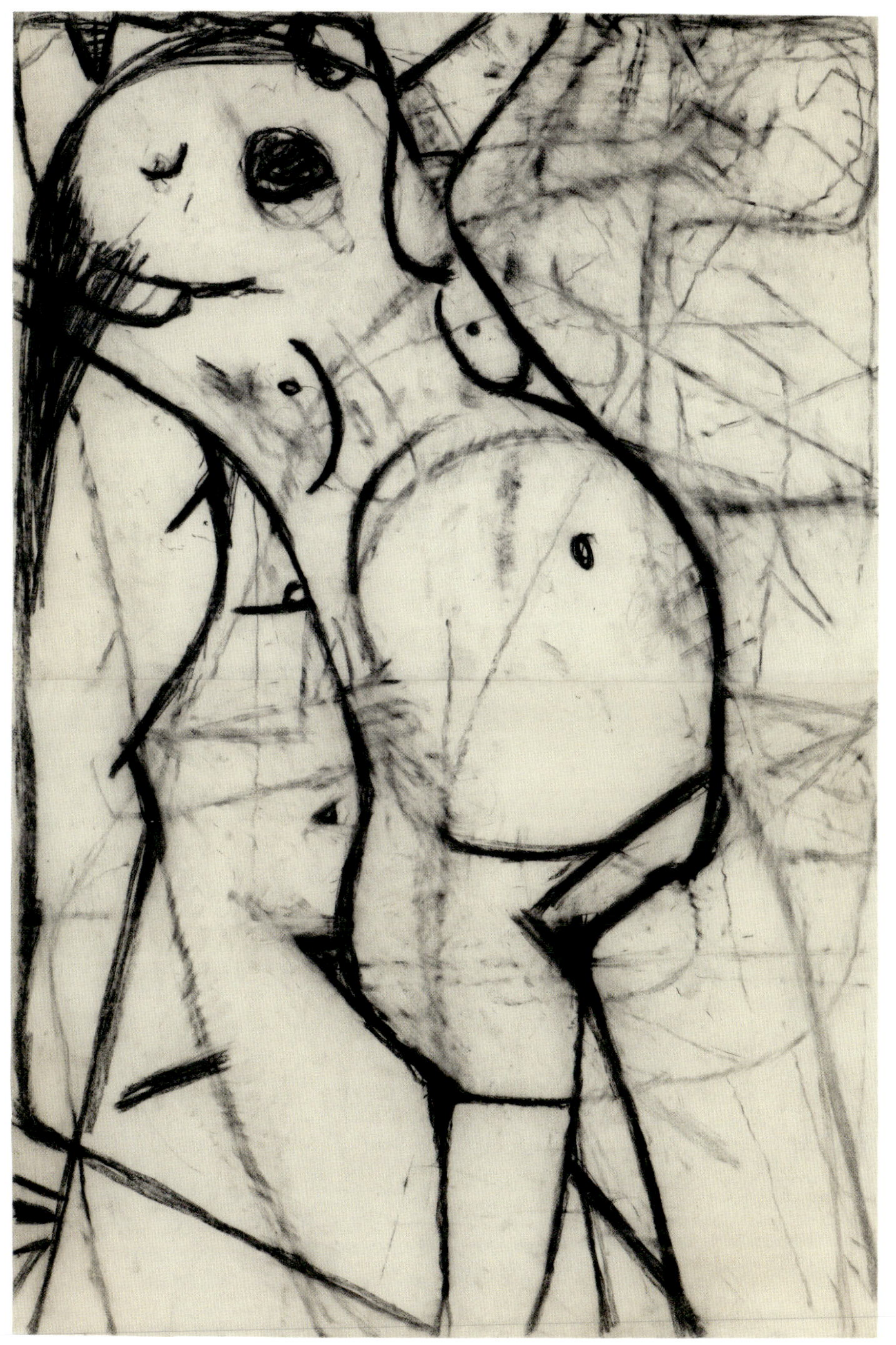

Untitled [Nude], 1956
Charcoal on paper
47.5 × 62.5 cm | 18¾ × 24⅝ in

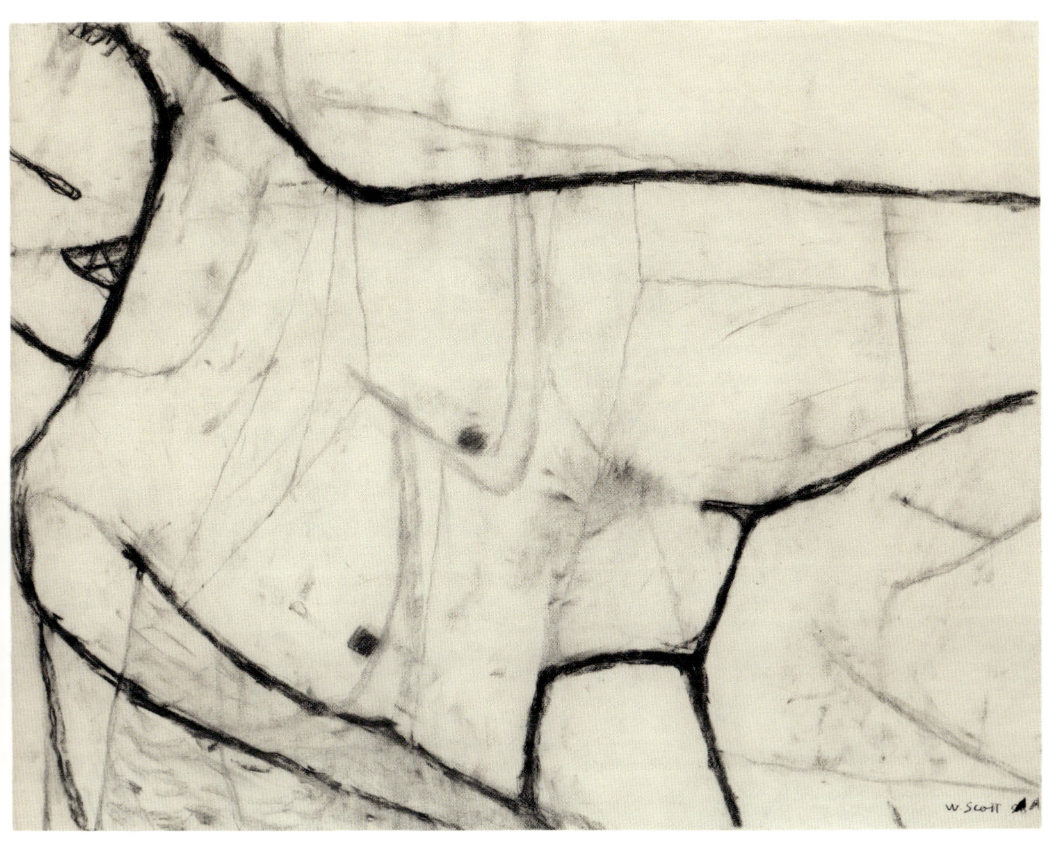

Seated Woman, 1953
Charcoal on paper
62.8 × 47.5 cm | 24¾ × 18¾ in

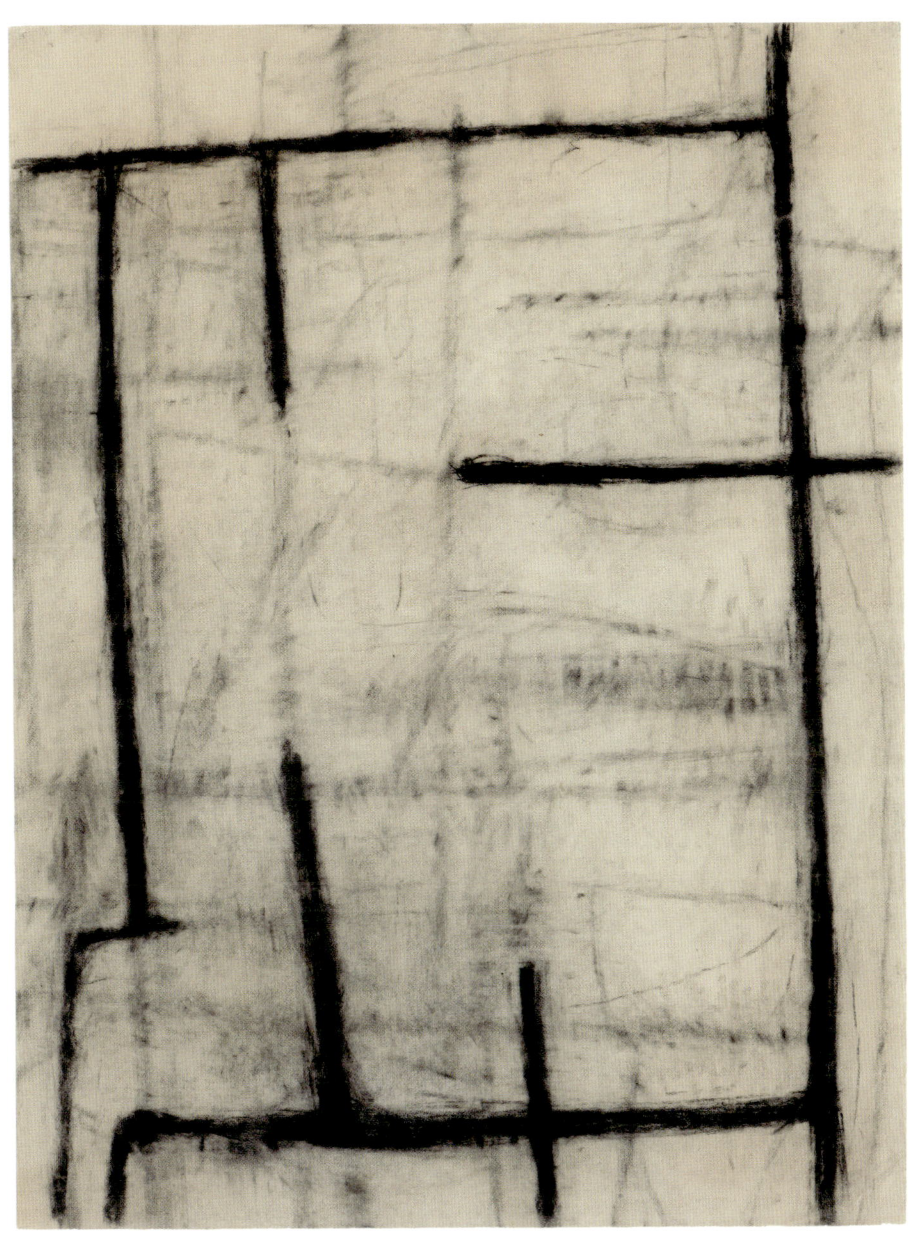

Study of a Nude, 1956
Charcoal on paper
20.3 × 25 cm | 8 × 9⅞ in

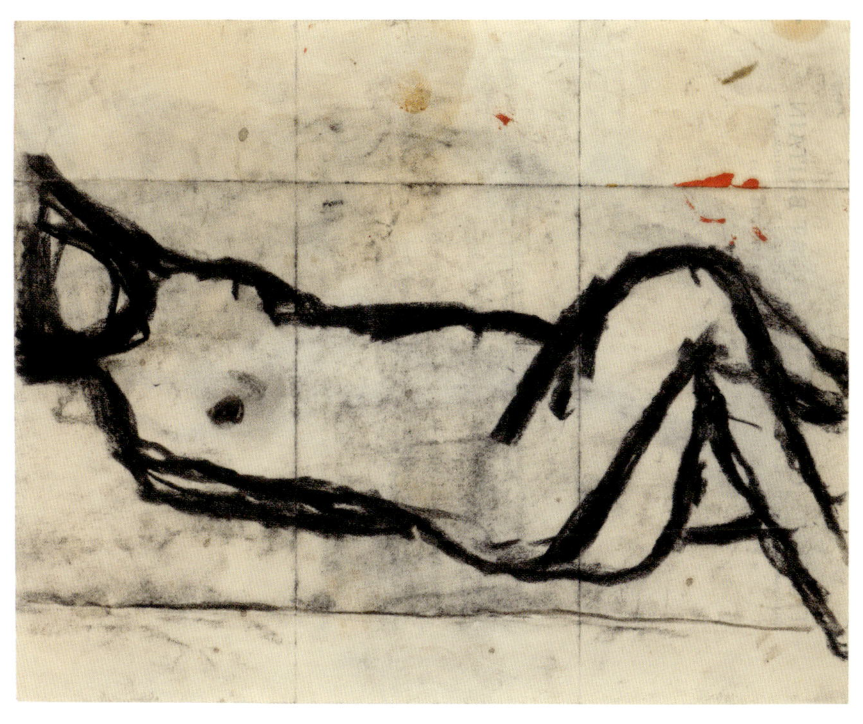

Untitled – Two Girls, 1956
Charcoal on paper
63 × 47.5 cm | 24¾ × 18¾ in

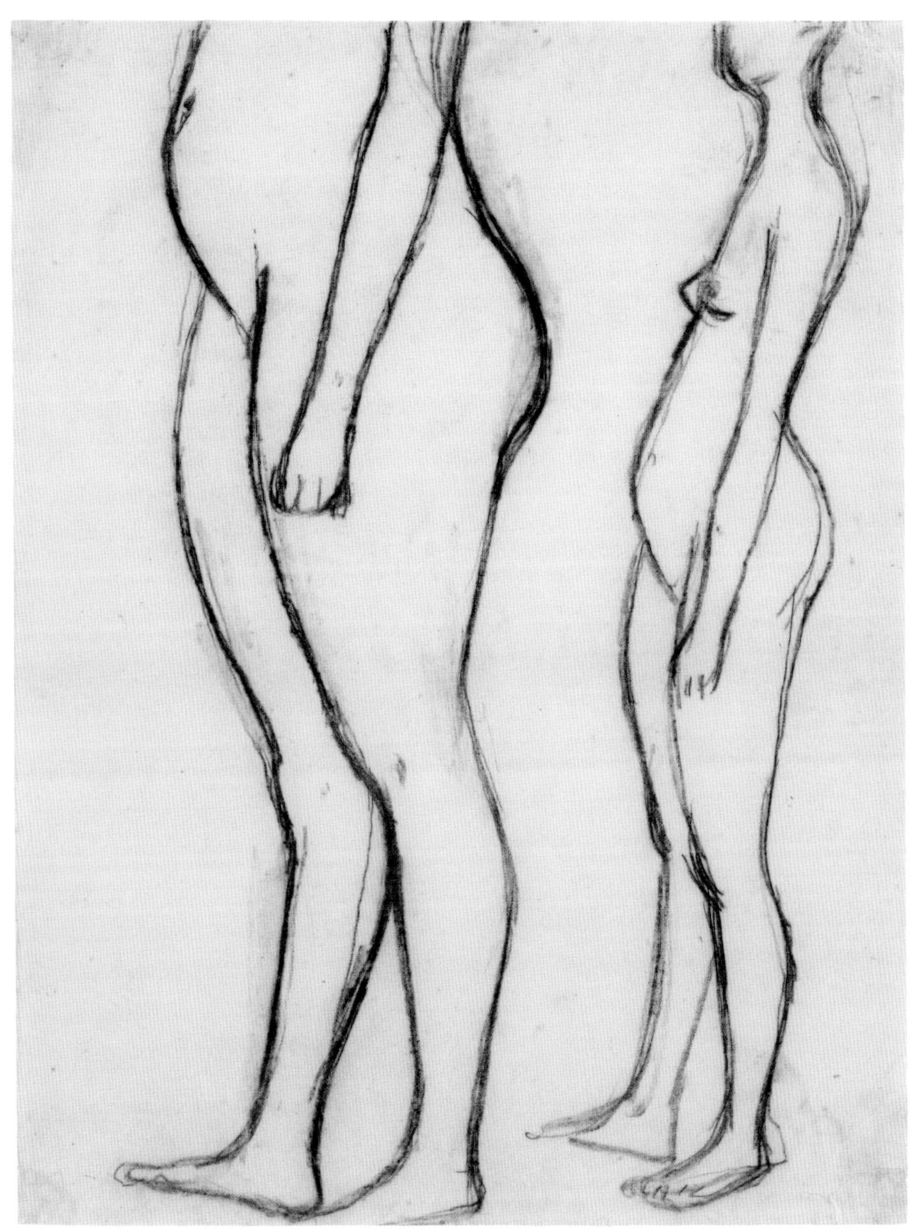

Untitled – Seated Nude, 1956
Charcoal on paper
47.7 × 62.6 cm | 18¾ × 24⅝ in

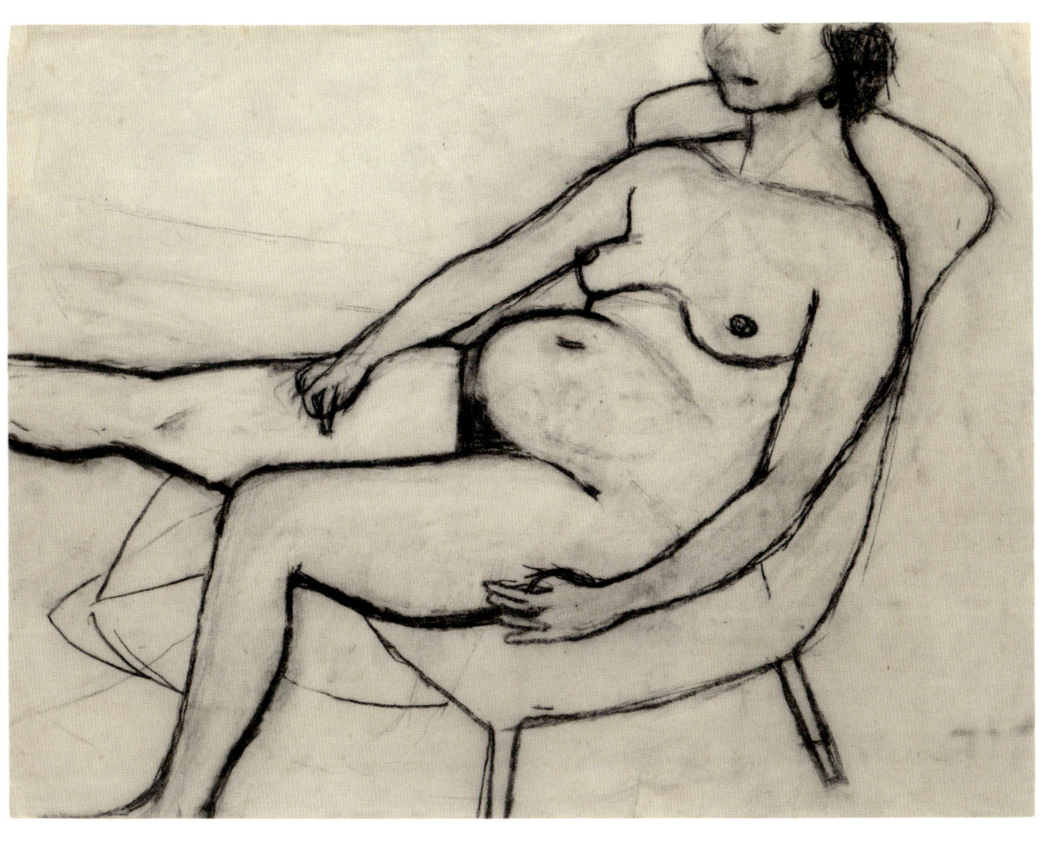

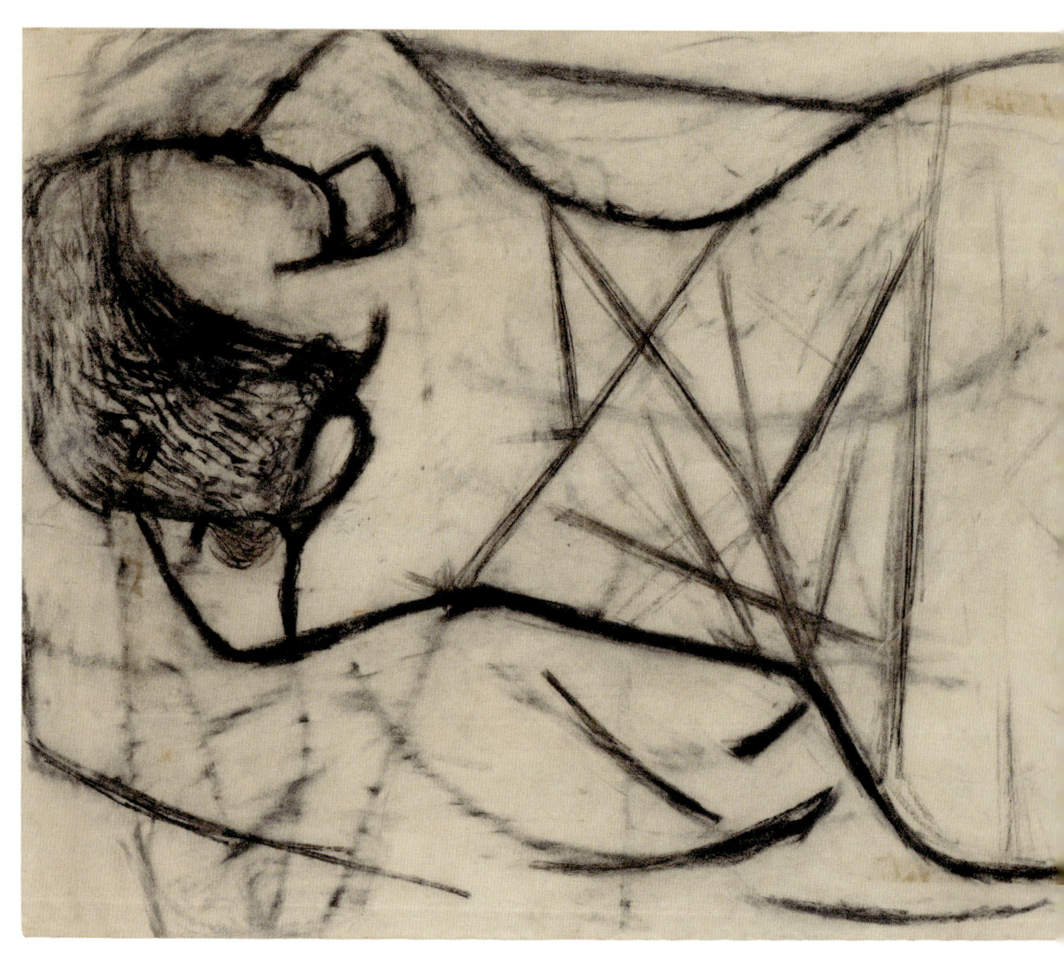

Girl Reclined No 1, 1956
Charcoal on paper
48 × 119 cm | 18⅞ × 46⅞ in

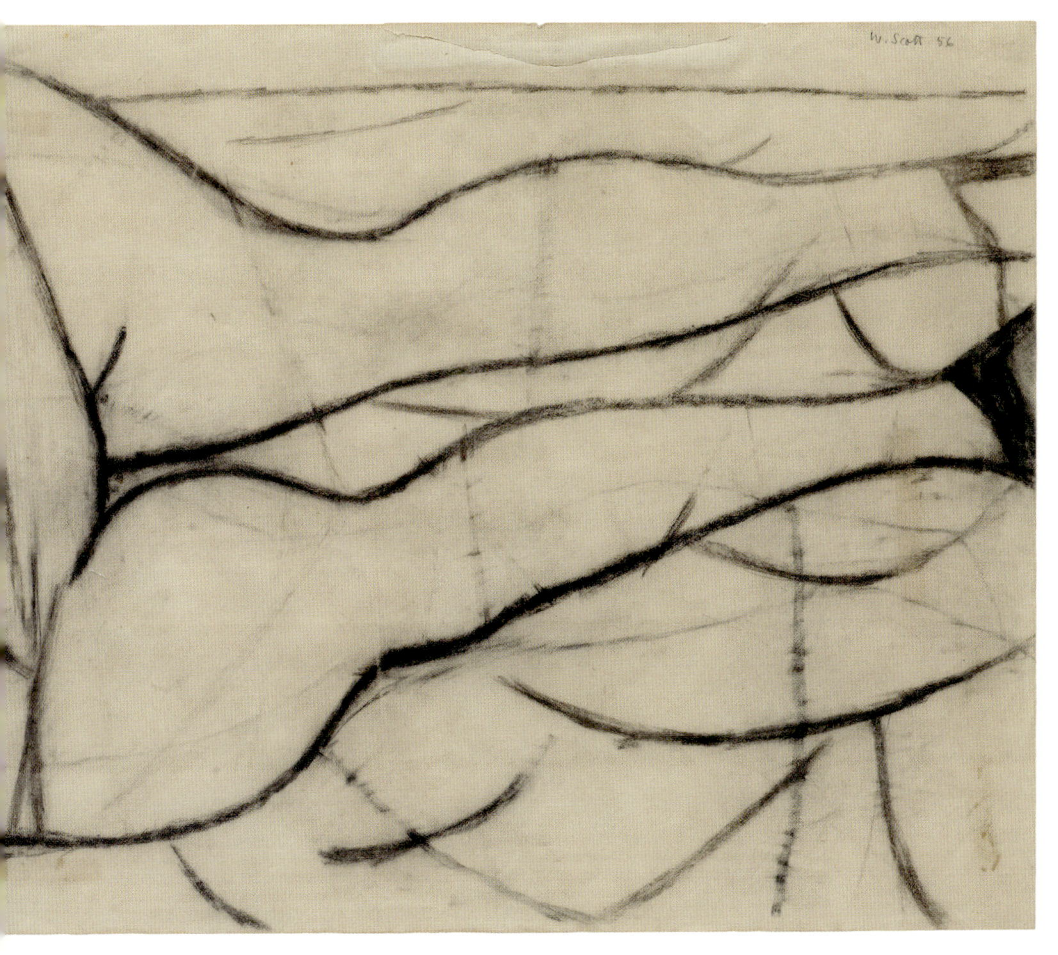

W. Scott 56

Untitled – Reclining Nude, 1956
Charcoal on paper
47.5 × 62.5 cm | 18¾ × 24⅝ in

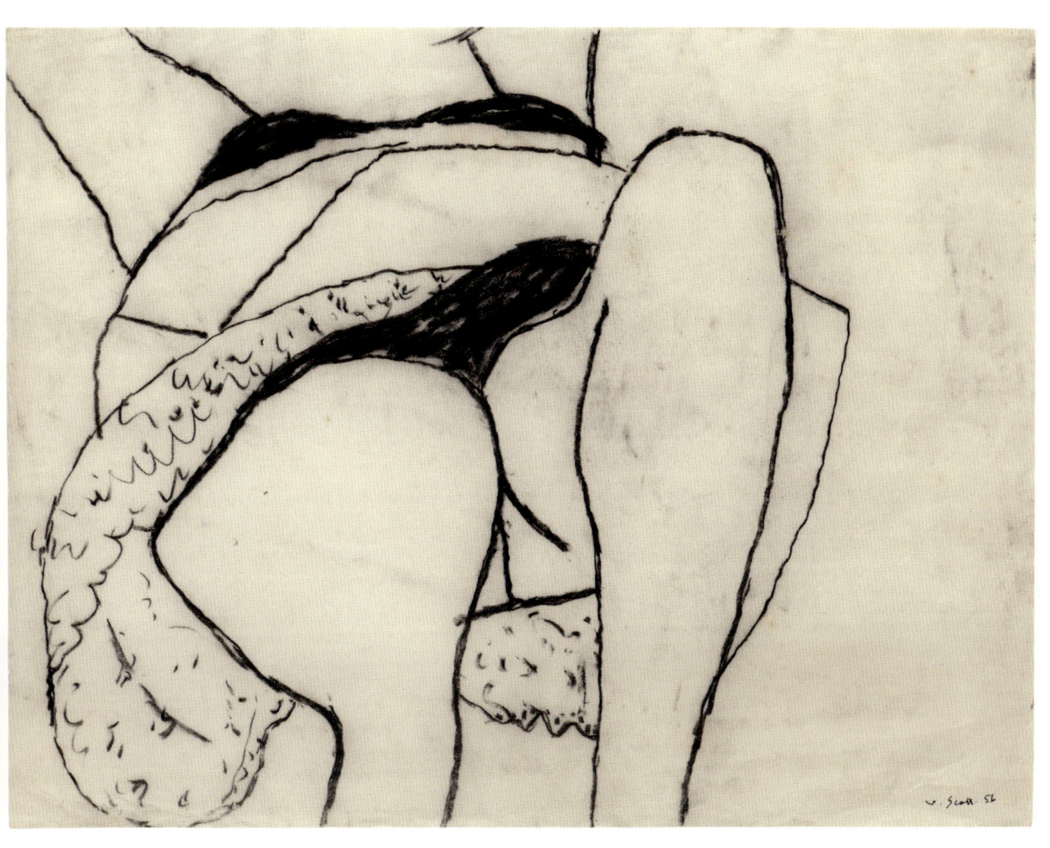

Cross Channel, 1957
Charcoal on paper
74.2 × 104.2 cm | 29¼ × 41⅛ in

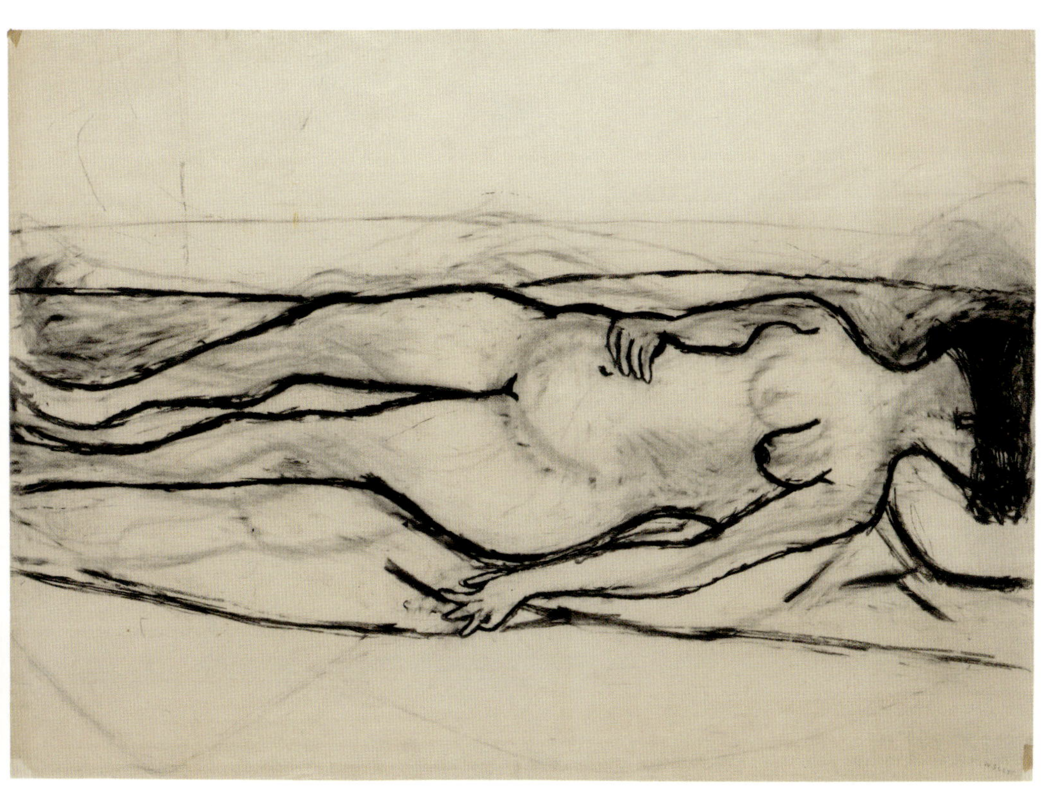

Untitled – Seated Nude, 1956
Charcoal on paper
47.5 × 63 cm | 18¾ × 24¾ in

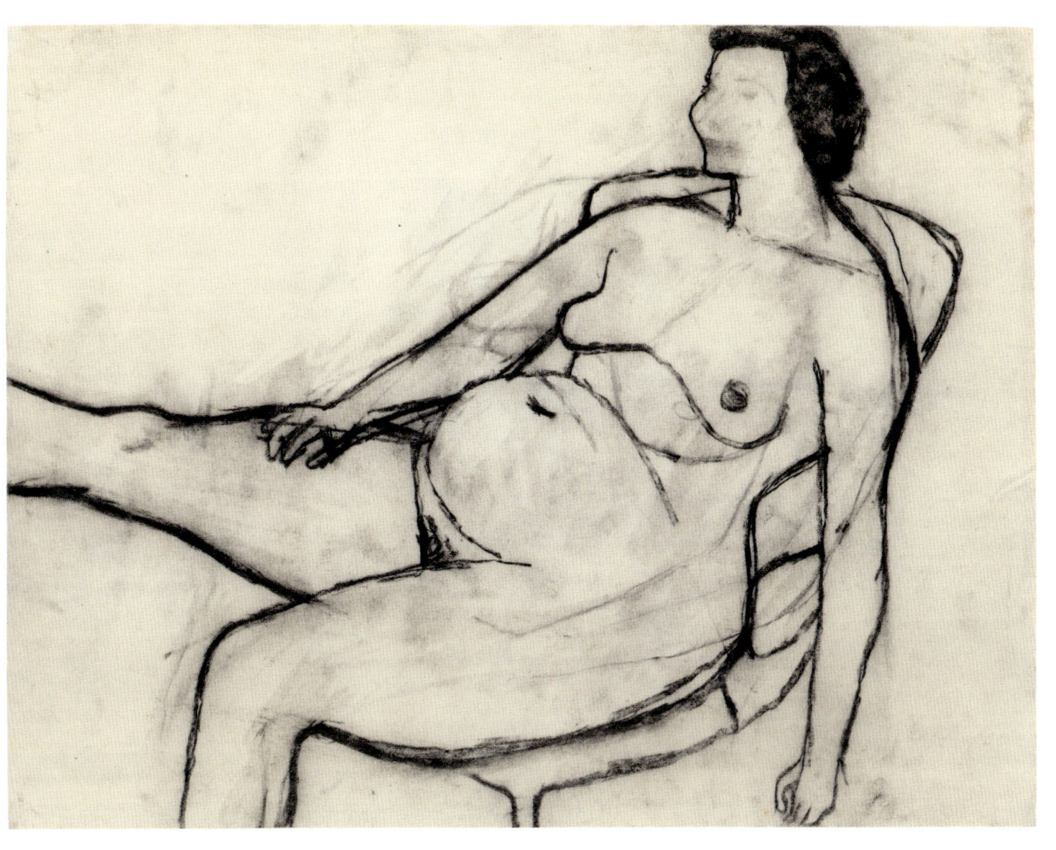

Untitled – Reclining Nude, 1956
Charcoal on paper
48.5 × 61 cm | 19 × 24⅛ in

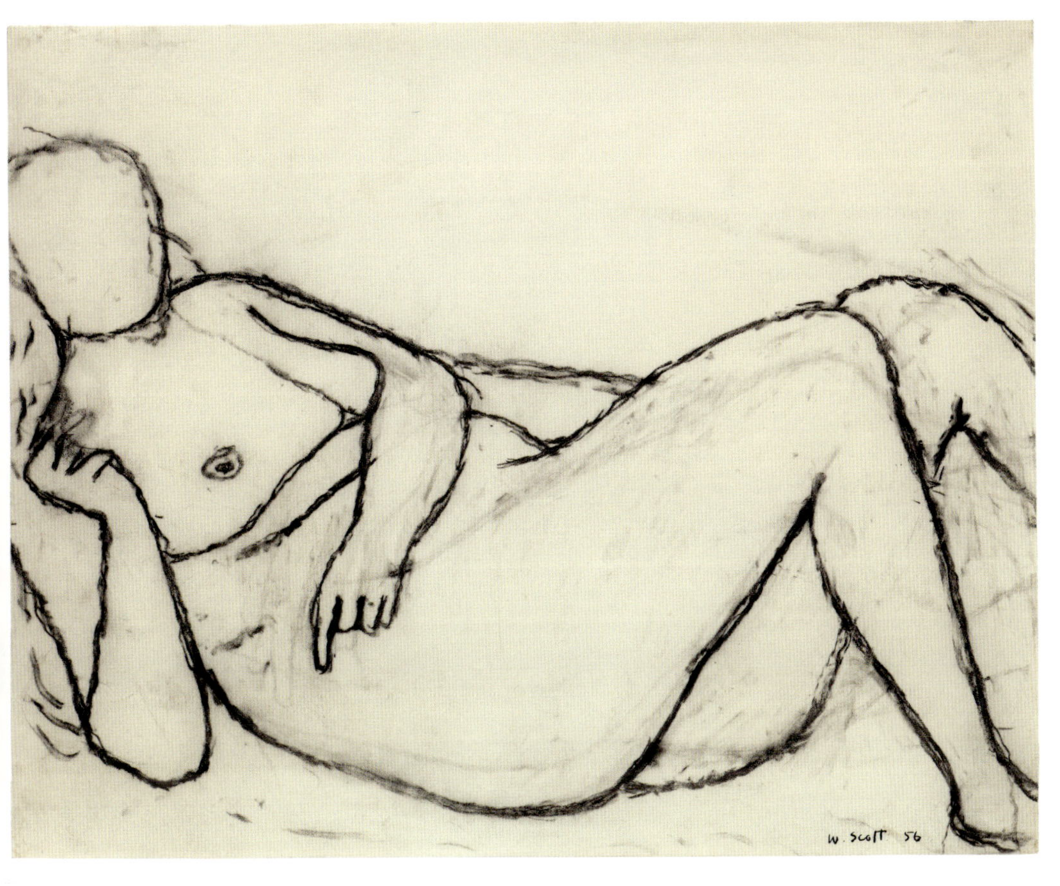

W. Scott 56

Seated Woman, 1954
Charcoal on paper
62.5 × 47.7 cm | 24 ⅝ × 18 ¾ in

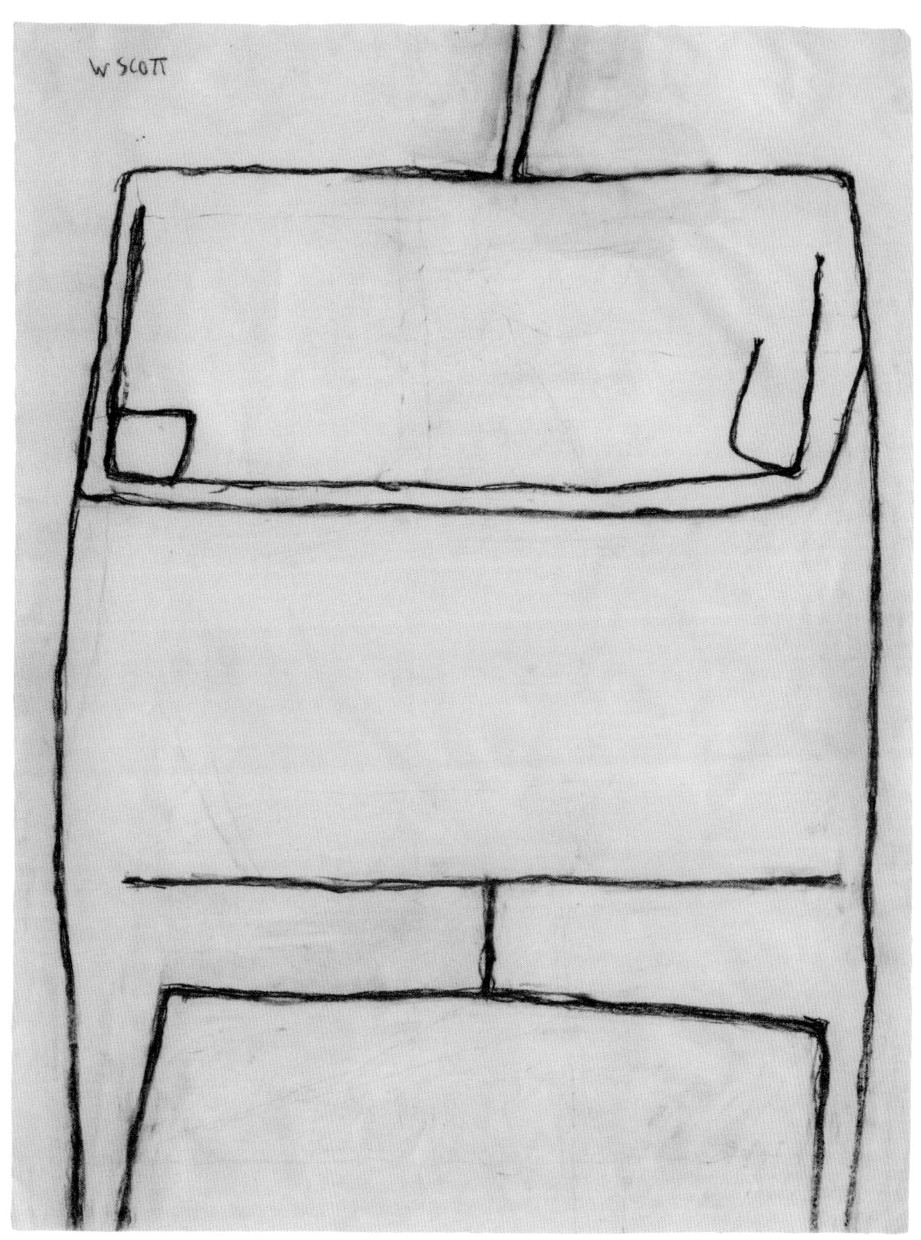

W SCOTT

Untitled – Reclining Nude, 1956
Charcoal on paper
47.8 × 62.5 cm | 18⅞ × 24⅝ in

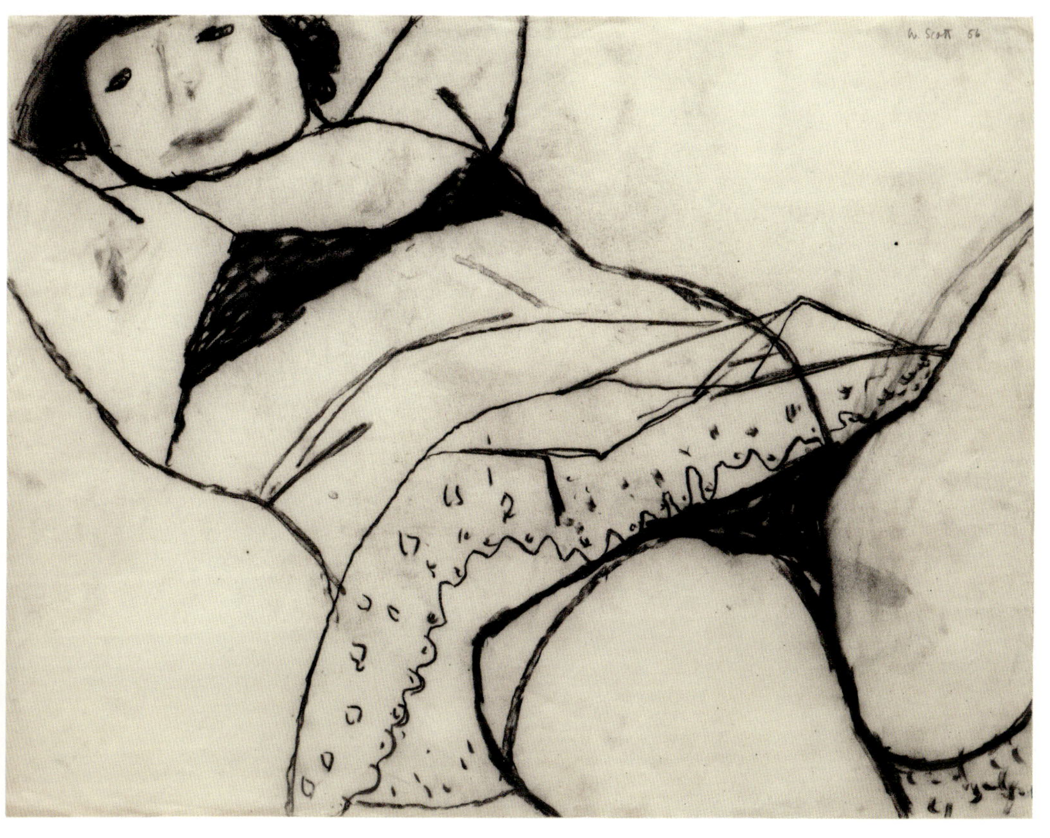

W. Scott 56

Study for a Painting, 1953
Charcoal on paper
61 × 49 cm | 24⅛ × 19¼ in

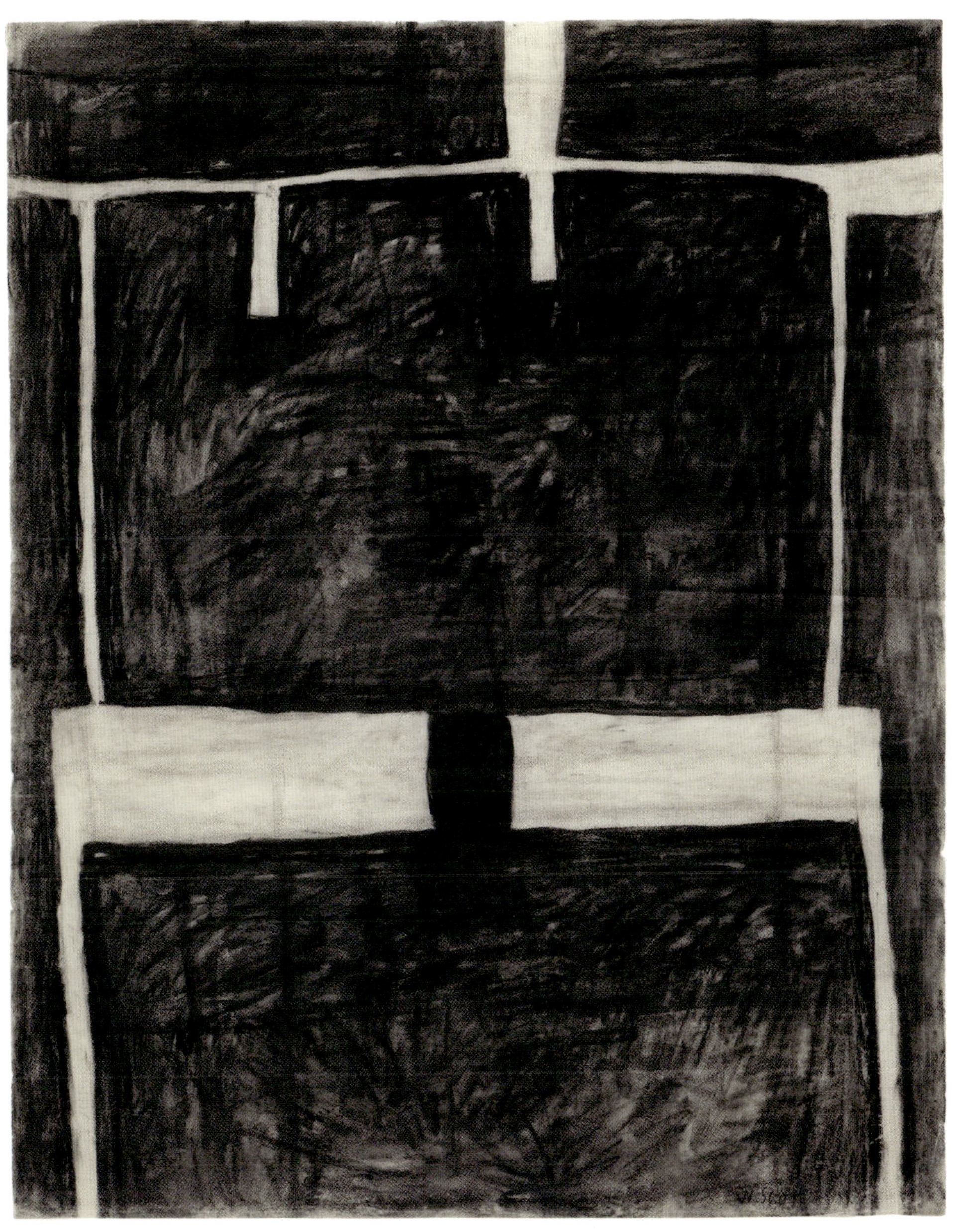

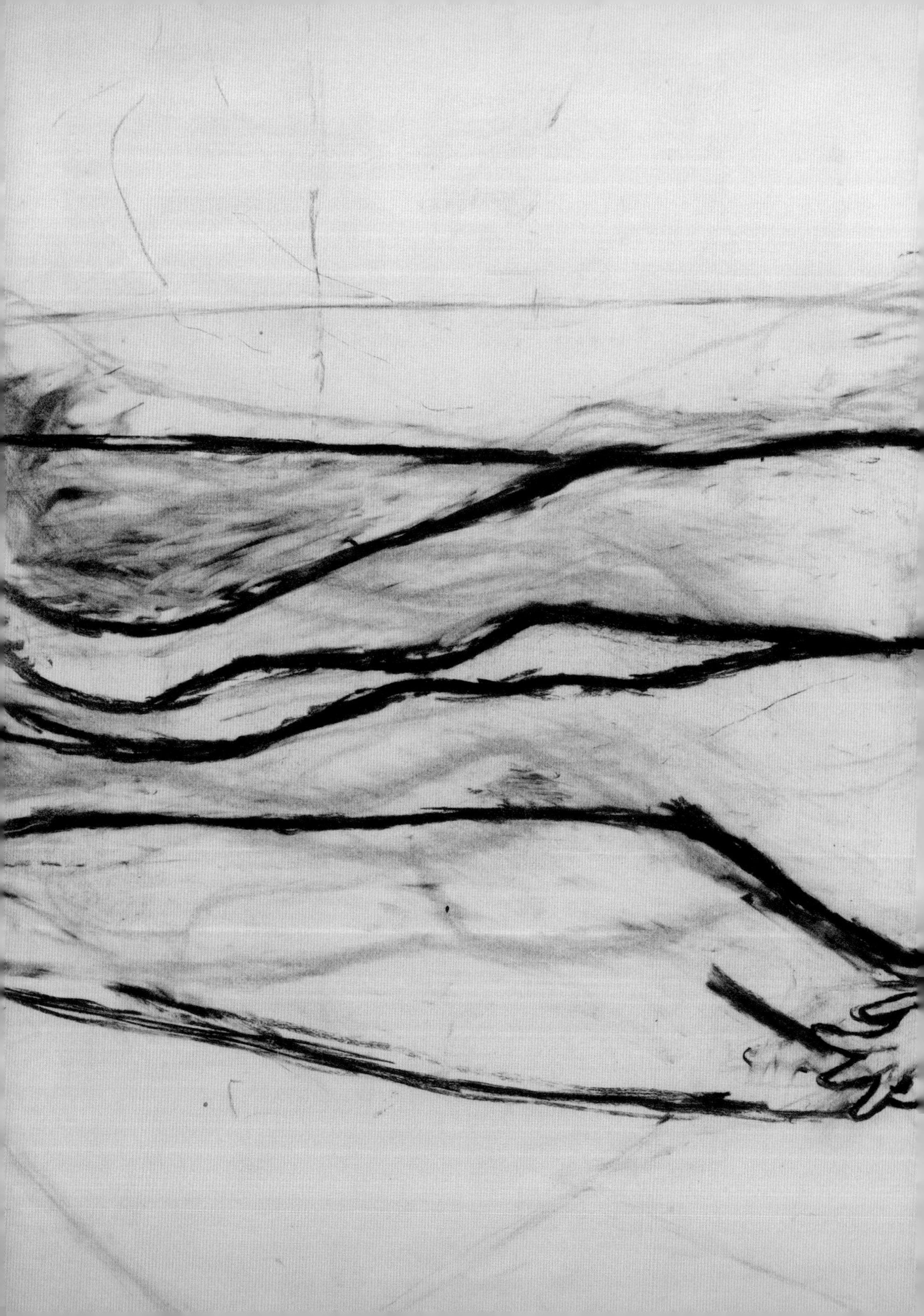

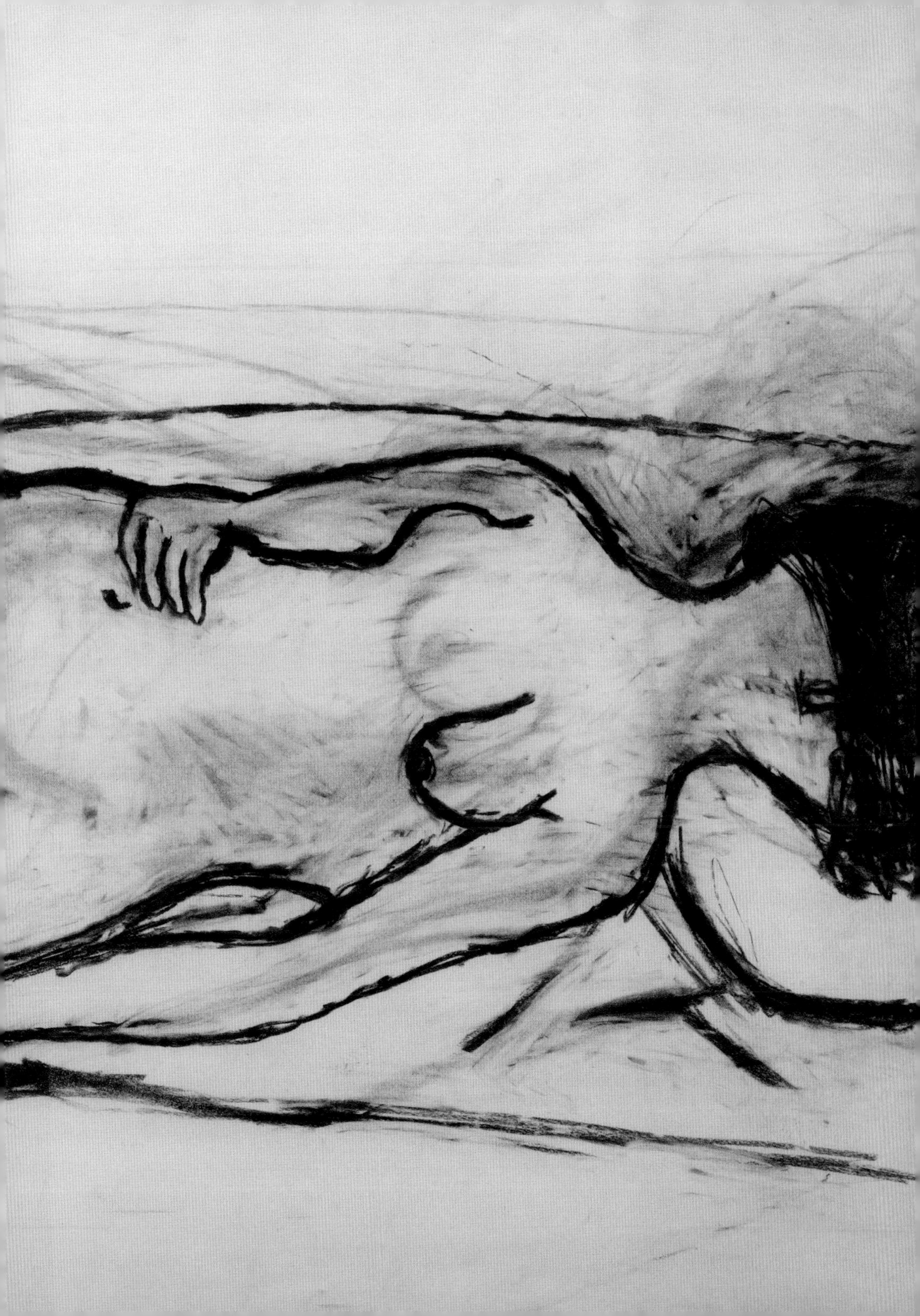

List of works

PAGES 28–29

Girl Reclined No 1, 1956

Charcoal on paper

48 × 119 cm | 18⅞ × 46⅞ in

EXHIBITED

Martha Jackson Gallery, New York, 1975

Albright-Knox Art Gallery, Buffalo, 1975

William & Mary Scott Related Drawings, Sculpture
    and Paintings, Enniskillen Castle, Fermanagh,
    29 September – 4 December, 1997, no.23

William Scott: Paintings and Drawings, Irish
    Museum of Modern Art, Dublin,
    22 July – 1 November, 1998, no.36, ill.

William Scott Book Launch at Air Gallery, Dover
    Street, London, 12–14 October, 2004

LITERATURE

Norbert Lynton, William Scott, Thames &
    Hudson, London, 2004, pl.269, pp.402–3.

PAGE 23

Study of a Nude, 1956

Charcoal on paper

20.3 × 25 cm | 8 × 9⅞ in

LITERATURE

Sarah Whitfield, William Scott: Catalogue Raisonné
    of Oil Paintings, Vol.2, Thames & Hudson,
    London, 2013, p.172.

PAGE 31

Untitled – Reclining Nude, 1956

Charcoal on paper

47.5 × 62.5 cm | 18¾ × 24⅝ in

EXHIBITED

William Scott: Paintings and Drawings, Irish
    Museum of Modern Art, Dublin,
    22 July – 1 November, 1998, no.25, ill.

PAGE 41

Untitled – Reclining Nude, 1956

Charcoal on paper

47.8 × 62.5 cm | 18⅞ × 24⅝ in

PAGE 37

Untitled – Reclining Nude, 1956

Charcoal on paper

48.5 × 61 cm | 19 × 24⅛ in

PAGE 17

Untitled – Nude, 1956

Charcoal on paper

94.5 × 62.5 cm | 37¼ × 24⅝ in

PAGE 35

Untitled – Seated Nude, 1956

Charcoal on paper

47.5 × 63 cm | 18¾ × 24¾ in

PAGE 27

Untitled – Seated Nude, 1956

Charcoal on paper

47.7 × 62.6 cm | 18¾ × 24⅝ in

EXHIBITED

William & Mary Scott Related Drawings, Sculpture
    and Paintings, Enniskillen Castle, Fermanagh,
    29 September – 4 December, 1997, no ill.

PAGE 25

Untitled – Two Girls, 1956

Charcoal on paper

63 × 47.5 cm | 24¾ × 18¾ in

PAGE 19

Untitled [Nude], 1956

Charcoal on paper

47.5 × 62.5 cm | 18¾ × 24⅝ in

PAGE 33

Cross Channel, 1957

Charcoal on paper

74.2 × 104.2 cm | 29¼ × 41⅛ in

EXHIBITED

Belfast, Dublin and Edinburgh, 1986, no.84

William & Mary Scott Related Drawings, Sculpture
    and Paintings, Enniskillen Castle, Fermanagh,
    29 September – 4 December, 1997, no.25

Published in 2013 by **Ridinghouse**
on the occasion of the exhibition

William Scott
1950s Nude Drawings
at Karsten Schubert, London
17 May – 12 July 2013

Ridinghouse
5–8 Lower John Street
London W1F 9DR
United Kingdom
www.ridinghouse.co.uk

Distributed in the UK and Europe by
Cornerhouse
70 Oxford Street
Manchester M1 5NH
United Kingdom
www.cornerhouse.org

Distributed in the US by
RAM Publications
2525 Michigan Avenue Building A2
Santa Monica, CA 90404
United States
www.rampub.com

British Library Cataloguing-in-Publication Data:
A full catalogue record of this book is available
from the British Library

ISBN 978 1 905464 75 3

Ridinghouse Publisher: Doro Globus
Editorial Assistant: Louisa Green
Designed by Tim Harvey
Set in Seria Sans
Printed in Italy by Studio Fasoli

Many thanks to Sarah Whitfield and the
William Scott Archive